INDEXICALITY

INDEXICALITY
An Africological Method of Inquiry

FUNTUNMFUNAFU DUA

Symbol of democracy and unity. The "Siamese crocodiles"
share one stomach, yet they fight over food.

INDEXICALITY

An Africological Method of Inquiry

Molefi Kete Asante, PhD

Little Black Book Series

RESEARCH METHODOLOGY, THEORY, AND PRAXIS

Volume 1

Series Editor: Serie McDougal, III, PhD

Universal Write Publications, LLC
New York, NY

INDEXICALITY: AN AFRICOLOGICAL METHOD OF INQUIRY

Library of Congress Control Number: 2025905448

PRINT: ISBN: 978-1-942774-50-1
eBOOK: ISBN: 978-1-942774-51-8

Printed in the United States of America.

Mailing/Submissions:

Universal Write Publications, LLC
421 8th avenue, Suite 86
New York, NY 10116

Website: UWPBooks.com

This book has been partially supported with a financial grant from SAGE Publishing.

S Sage

Preface

Each discipline has its own identification markers. If there are no markers for the discipline, then there is no discipline. The character of a discipline is to have footprints that allow those who wish to study its theories and methods to follow its pathways in acquiring knowledge. I have spent five decades extending the boundaries of the discipline of Africology by interrogating the practices of the best Afrocentric scholars. Some of these scholars, to be sure, have been my own students who have explored their own routes to a more robust theory or set of procedures for research. I have always been happy with this type of development because it demonstrates that the field of Africology is not a religion and does not demand faith. It is rather an arena for debate, discussion, and practice, all in search for the most useful way to explain phenomena related to the African world. The Africological study of society, art, science, philosophy, communication, the mind, economics, and the future are within the purview of the discipline of Africology.

I employ the term *indexicality* to capture the nature of the process that allows researchers to make sense of the world Africologically. The kiSwahili word *"ripoti"* is translated as index in English. The quality of *ripoti* is indexicality, that is, the active discovery of markers within the cultural, social, economic, or spiritual profile of the phenom. *A phenom in Africology is any event, person, concept, or action that can be apprehended and put to explanatory use* (Asante, 2007). One can inquire into the nature of mental states, economic realities, historical realities, social behaviors, cultural aesthetic formations, and exhibitions to secure understanding from an Afrocentric perspective. My effort in this small book is to point to scopes, procedures, and maps for inquiry.

Over the past six or more decades since the first department of Black Studies emerged at San Francisco State University in 1966, our obligation as scholars has been to create theory and methods for research in Africology (Asante, 1987). We often found that our early methods were derived from the traditional European disciplines in which we had been educated (Asante & Welsh Asante, 1990). We had no issue with data since the acquisition of data had already been worked on by historians, sociologists, psychologists, and political scientists, and new procedures were always being discovered for unveiling hidden or unrevealed information. There were those African scholars in the Americas who did history but were not named as historians. Some were called lay historians or "old scrappers"; that is, they were people who delved into sources to discover facts about African and African American life but had no professional training (Bernal, 1987). Such was the work of J. A. Rogers, John Henrik Clarke, and Yosef ben Jochannon, outstanding students of history, science, and society capable of making innovative interpretations of data (Clarke, 1991; Jochannon, 1972; Rogers, 1972). So historical data existed, and experimental and behavior data were being collected by psychologists (McDougal, 2014). Our problem was that we had no methods to go with the nascent theories that we had developed by reading the works of Cheikh Anta Diop, Chancellor Williams, Ivan van Sertima, George G. M. James, Theophile Obenga, Nathan Hare, Asa Hilliard, and Marimba Ani (Ani, 1994; Clarke, 1991; Diop, 1974; Jochannon, 1972; Rogers, 1972; Williams, 1993). Sometimes, these scholars, while trained at the best universities, were overlooked or ignored by Eurocentric scholars who had no clue about African or African

American giants who investigated Africa as well as critiqued Europe.

This small book will provide approaches to apprehending data, facts, and interpretations of reality from an Africological basis, but more than that this work is a celebration of the kind of research, explorations, and studies carried out by African scholars who have brought a new analysis to old data. This work is not sociology, political science, urban studies, psychology, or history, yet in some ways, the information utilized might suggest similar methods found in other disciplines. The first course should always be to discover what is consistent with the principal theories in our field. It is important that we open encourage new confrontations with sources, analyses, and interpretations to effect the changes in the field that we know are important for understanding racial, class, gender issues. Obviously from my own reading of the texts and the research, I have found the following theories and concepts as the most abundant in the literature produced by scholars in Africology.

SOME THEORIES USED BY AFRICOLOGY SCHOLARS

Theorist	Theory	Key Concepts	Book
Molefi Kete Asante	Afrocentricity	Agency, Centeredness	The Afrocentric Idea
W. Cross	Nigrescence	Blackness	Shades of Black
George Dei	Anti-Racism	Equity	Playing the Race Card
Derrida	Deconstruction	Fluidity	Writing and Difference
Nah Dove	African Womanism	Maaticity	Afrikan Mothers
Henry Louis Gates	Signifying	Signification	The Signifying Monkey
C. Hudson-Weems	Africana Womanism	Complementarity	Africana Womanism

Theorist	Theory	Key Concepts	Book
Maulana Karenga	Kawaida	Culture, Maat	*Maat: The Moral Idea in Ancient Egypt*
K. Marx	Marxism	Class	*Communist Manifesto*
Lewis Gordon	Black Existentialism	Critique, domination	*Black Existentialism*
Kwame Nkrumah	Consciencism	African Personality	*Consciencism*
J.P. Sartre	Existentialism	Decision	*Being and Nothingness*
R. Anderson	Black Speculative Arts	Time, technology, and Space	
F. Saussure	Structuralism	Formalism	*Course in General Linguistics*
L. Senghor	Negritude	Emotion, Feeling	*Negritude et Humanisme*
Christel Temple	Mythology	Cultural Memory	*Black Cultural Mythology*
K. Welsh Asante	Nzuri	Recognition	*African Aesthetic*

I am aware that the preceding list is incomplete since new theories and concepts are being developed in areas of the discipline that I may not know, but I present this as a heuristic only to be enlarged and developed further by readers. A researcher could explore any one of these or other theories for analytical and explanatory value. For example, the work being carried out by Reynaldo Anderson and others in Afrofuturism and Black Speculative Arts will soon yield new ideas and concepts in Africology (Anderson, 2016, 2025). One must see that Aaron Smith's enlargement of the Afrofuturist idea to Afrocentric futurism will at some point converge with the previous works in this field and will allow researchers to explore various ways to maximize Afrocentricity as a tool for innovation (Smith, 2023).

I am interested in drawing inferences from the actual research carried out by those who claim to be Afrocentric scholars. The best way to write about methods is to see what others in the field have made to extend the way we view reality. Thus, I want to present fundamental material not usually found in research books to show how researchers might approach conundrums of African phenomena. I will use examples from the scholarship of Afrocentrists to demonstrate what methods have been useful in discovering new knowledge and interpretations about African phenomena (Banks, 1996). There is no way that this book can describe all the different methods applied by Afrocentrists since there are now more than 200 scholars who have gained doctorate degrees as Afrocentrists; at best, I hope to point toward directions that might be exploited by innovative researchers who are seeking to climb out of the epistemic cave created by Eurocentrists. We have been joined in this work by scholars like Kgothatso B. Shai, Simphiwe Sesanti, Mogomme Masoga, Vusi Gumede, and Lehasa Moloi of South Africa who are questioning the old traditions of European research methods when applied to African issues (Moloi, 2024; Sesanti, 2019; Shai, 2024). It must be clear that Afrocentric methods are not tied to any ethnic identity. Anyone with an open mind can apply the necessary protocols, ask the proper questions, and make the critical interrogations necessary to overcome the chains around our brains and break down the walls. Everywhere there is a challenge to the wall constructed by the Pan European Academy. Books and articles have appeared with titles like *An Afrocentric Idea on Contested Knowledge*, "Seven Days in May: An Afrocentric Diagnosis of Shepherd Mpofu's Facebook Roar," "An Afro-Decolonial Critique of China's Response to South Africa's Development Priorities, 2009–2017," "Afrocentric Critique of World Systems Analysts as a Critical Theory in International

Relations," "An Afrocentric Critique of South Africa's Contemporary Knowledge Production Regime," and scores of other books and articles from all over the world. Now that there are papers and journals in Brazil, Russia, Greece, Japan, China, and France examining the nature of an Afrocentric approach to knowledge production there will continue to be a growing need for new epistemologies, ontologies, and paradigms that are detached from the influences of those who have sought to inferiorize Africans for centuries.

Contents

CHAPTER 1
Breaking the Walls

Eurocentrism emerged out of the West as a religious, explorative, exploitative, assertive, imperial agency with the purpose of aggressively advancing the gospel of white racial supremacy in all sciences and arts. In so doing, it established a wall of exclusivity where the only theorists were white and the only researchers with legitimacy were those who followed the pattern laid down by those inside of the Pan European Academy's wall (Akua, 2012; Asante, 2020). Our inclination as Africologists is to break the wall to have a clearer view of African phenomena.

STEPS TOWARD A EUROPEAN WALL

When Charles Martel marshaled the Christian tribes in Gaul and surrounding areas to defend the Christian kingdoms at the Battle of Tours, often called Battle of Poitiers, from the Moorish army, he initiated the idea of a European commonality, and its subsequent Eurocentrism, which has become an ethnocentric idea, meant to advance European superiority by going "into all the world" as a part of its imperial and colonial impetus. As the Afrocentric theorist, Maulana Karenga has stated and emphasized one gathers from Eurocentrism that is a hierarchical system founded on the notion of race and deeply endowed with overtones of white racial and religious domination (Karenga, 2003, pp. 141–160).

It is this system that has expanded to a global project. For me, Eurocentrism is an aggressive, globalized, and racialized Judeo-Christian ideology with heteronormative, capitalist, and colonial inclination. No Africological research should undergird this drive for inequality and the lack of diversity. I see our task as one that must challenge all forms of ideological and mental deformations that seek to create galaxies of ignorance by parading as economic, social, and political authorities. Sabelo Gatsheni-Ndlovu argues that Eurocentrism is "a Euro-North American theory of human history which privileges the Greek-Roman classical world as the cradle of human civilization. In the process it overshadowed the reality of Africa as the certified cradle of humankind … fashioning Africans as people without souls, a people without religion, a people without history, a people without civilization, a people without development, a people without democracy, a people without human rights, and people without ethics—a corrupt people. The list is endless. The result of the labels was gradual and cumulative loss of ontological density by Black people" (Ndlovu-Gatsheni, 2015). Certainly, Eurocentrism can impact the production of knowledge and the methods by which we produce it. Our aim is to align our research to a production of knowledge that supports our purpose of making a better, more compassionate world; otherwise, we are condemned to the distortions, mistakes, and abuses of the Hegelian or Eurocentric ideal.

HOW THE WALL WAS BUILT

To prosecute the maligning of Africa, it was necessary for Hegel, the greatest European thinker since Plato, to advance a false division of the continent, a division superimposed on the land, not by the people of the continent themselves but by European historians, anthropologists, and colonial administrators who said Africa consisted of Asian Africa, European Africa, and Africa proper. In *Philosophy of History*, he explained that Africa proper was the territory south of the Sahara; European Africa was the territory north of the Sahara; Egypt was the part of Africa connected to Asia (Hegel, 1956). This division is arbitrary and has no validity in point of fact. Africa is geographically and culturally, due to natural barriers, more continental than Europe. There is neither an Africa north of the Sahara nor south of the Sahara as Hegel claimed; the Sahara is Africa, and human populations have inhabited the Sahara for thousands of years. It is as useless to speak of Africa separated by deserts, as it is to speak of separations by rain forests. What Hegel and others of his school of thought have attempted to argue since the emergence of the Aryan model is that Africa in its northern areas was somehow different qualitatively from Africa in the southern areas. This is why Hegel could say of Africa that it was "a land of childhood, which lying beyond the day of self-conscious history, is enveloped in the dark mantle of night" (Hegel, 1956). Such commentary shows an extreme disregard for the historical processes carried out by Africans in various cultural and social contexts for many millennia. Indeed, Egypt, the grandest civilization of antiquity, was necessarily seen in Hegel's view as belonging more to Arabic influences than African, even though African civilization in Egypt had flourished 4,000 years prior to the coming of the Arabs.

Hegel must have been aware of the contradictory bases of his discussion of African geography. One cannot assert the continental definition of Africa geographically while trying to deny Africa's unity culturally by insisting that the "real Africa" is only a portion of the continent. European Africa, of course, never existed and was merely the Hegelian attempt to Germanicize all those people who may have contributed to African coastal civilizations. Hegel's claims for northern Africa being European or Asian are no more to be accepted or believed than someone else's claims that southern Europe was African Europe. Cheikh Anta Diop is most authoritative on this question, contending that a Black African people occupied the northern part of the African continent since "prehistoric" times.

As to Egypt being connected to Asia as Hegel claims without any evidence, Diop is most clear:

> ... if a civilization comparable to that of Egypt had flowered there [in Asia] ... its memory, no matter how vague, would have been transmitted to us by the Ancients, who form one branch of the Indo-Europeans, who furnished so many corroborative testimonials on the Negro-Egyptian culture. (Diop, 1974, p. 102)

What is more certain, however, is the intimate connection of ancient Egypt with Nubia, Punt, Libya, and Ethiopia (Monges, 1995). Since the Nile River is the principal organ of Egyptian social, historical, civic, and monumental life, is not it natural that the civilizations of the Nile Valley would be more closely related to ancient Egypt than more distant and less accessible lands?

Perhaps one of the most revealing statements in the *Philosophy of History* is Hegel's assurance that "among the Negroes moral sentiments are quite weak, or more strictly speaking, nonexistent" (Hegel, 1956). Such rhetoric was probably not unusual as the spirit of the time in Europe was one of racial expansionism and growing sentiments for the doctrine of Germanic racial supremacy. Morality would prove in both the 19th and 20th centuries not to be a special attribute reserved for Germanic peoples.

Hegel's place in Eurocentrism is supreme, and he joins Plato and Marx as the most influential thinkers in the European pantheon. But his speculative idealism in historical thinking has led to some permutations that have entrapped the best minds of Europe and

America. Without a doubt, Hegel's influence on sociology, history, political science, and philosophy remains prominent and insidious. Its prominence is seen in the quotations, allusions, and examples taken from his works by contemporary scholars; his insidiousness is found in the structure of thought found in the writings of European and American scholars. While it is true that Hegel's ideas on the Absolute, the world spirit, dialectics, and ethical idealism provoked some reaction in the works of the Marxists, Kierkegaard, G. E. Moore, and others, he nevertheless was seldom checked by his European critics or followers for his racist views regarding Africans or Asians. Furthermore, the works of Theodor Adorno and Herbert Marcuse, although rooted in Hegelian ideas and used for quite different purposes than Hegel may have appreciated, are valuable for their endeavor to forge new relevance out of Hegel's dialectic. Yet, clearly the Hegelian philosophy was responsible for the historicist crisis that led to Marx and Kierkegaard as opposed to a Goethean serenity based on the eternal return motif. Historicism itself owes a large debt to Hegel's influence. But historicism has raised numerous questions among philosophers and the ensuing debates have thrown light on the nature of the European anxiety over method. In many ways, this is a good thing because as Yoshitaka Miike has shown that the idea of rationality itself is often misleading in a discourse about world knowledge (Miike, 2019).

A DIFFERENT VIEW

Our methodology is holistic and integrative: our epistemology, participatory, and committed. The Africologist is a working scholar committed to the advancement of knowledge about the African world. In pursuing a vision in Afrocentric scholarship, the Africologist gathers facts about African phenomena, verifies them and subjects the interpretations to the strictest measures.

The aim of the Africologist is to make the world more meaningful to those who live in it and to create spaces for human understanding. Our task is not like that of the Western social scientist who seeks to predict human behavior to advance more direct control over nature but rather to explain human nature as it is manifested in the African arena. All statements about objects, phenomena, and events are subjects for discussion, analysis, and action. To be a good Africologist, the scholar must be able to distinguish between Afrocentric statements and less precise non-Afrocentric statements (Walters, 1990). In fact, we can say this is the first qualification for a researcher.

The following statements, with their obvious biases, are found in contemporary Eurocentric scholarly works.

Kenneth Clark once wrote and presented the following assessment on the BBC series on Civilization:

> ... Apollo embodies a higher state of civilization than the mask. They both represent spirits, messengers from another world.... To the negro imagination it is a world of fear and darkness, ready to inflict horrible punishment for the smallest infringement of a taboo to the Hellenistic imagination it is a world of light and confidence in which gods are like ourselves, only more beautiful, and descend to earth in order to teach men reason and the laws of harmony. (Clark, 1969)

One can find examples of this type of analysis throughout the Western world. For example, regarding the Aztec and Inca civilizations many Europeans have used terms such as "being forced to subjugate," "primitive peoples," and "more civilized." These terms indicate a perspective on the reality of conquest with guns, ships, cannons, and smallpox on the attack of indigenous peoples.

In these statements and sentiments by Eurocentric writers, one senses the bias against other cultures. Kenneth Clark, well respected as a major force in European culture, demonstrates his prejudice against African culture and his ignorance of African art. He chooses to compare the Apollo with the mask, any mask, rather than to compare the Apollo with the Ramses at Abu Simbel or some similar sculpture from African classical antiquity. His contrast of a world of fear and a world of confidence represents self-conscious attempts to valorize the European experience above the African. The fact is that anyone capable of manipulating language could play the same game. One surely would not compare Stonehenge with the Giza Pyramids or the Inzalo y'Langa in Mpumalanga, South Africa. The Spaniard assessment of conquest places prejudices not so much in *comparisons* as in *omissions* of understanding. Spanish destruction of other civilizations was not something that had to be done. The idea that Spaniards "*were forced to subjugate*" appears to be a euphemism. Furthermore, the indigenous civilizations are said to have "*disappeared*" when in fact someone *disappeared* them. A serious researcher must be aware of the context in which research or analysis takes place. As the Europeans promote the idea of a firm individuality, for example, the African idea is to encourage community and society as keys to cultural analysis.

An example I have used a lot is the one that involves southern and central Africa and the meeting of the missionary David Livingston and mercenary Henry Morton Stanley. Sometimes writers of history have concentrated on the meeting of these two white men in the African forest as history, even though they were amid thousands of people living at the same time and space. Africans are said to be without history. An intellectual dishonesty, perpetrated by racist historians, allowed history to be what happened to two Europeans among hundreds of thousands of Africans. Situated in the Neckar River Valley, separated from the wider world Hegel, and later Karl Jaspers, Jurgen Habermas and Hannah Arendt spent time contemplating the relationship of Germans and their culture to the rest of the world from their

perch at Heidelberg University. Hegel looked out from the philosopher's path and wrote nonsense about African people and
African history. In Hegelian terms, Africans are an obscure people, obscure in this instance because Europeans do not know
them but certainly not obscure to their own recorders, musi-
cians, historians, epics, myths, and chronicles. Africologists
cannot deny individual narratives, but they must be placed
within the context of the collective.

Hegel's position on Greece is like that of other European and
American writers; indeed, they view the Greek experience as a
virgin birth of their own experience; of course, in numerous
forms what has paraded as Greece derived is actually African
derived (James, 2017). Hegel's predicament is even more complex because in philosophy he demonstrates an awesome
ignorance of ancient African civilizations placing Egypt, even
currently, at the bottom of world civilizations. This was princi-
pally a Eurocentric reaction to an African civilization and since
Hegel did have the benefit of reading the work of the French
writers and scholars who wrote of the monumental nature of an
African civilization, he could admit, with reluctance, the anteri-
ority of Egypt, but he would not admit, even reluctantly, that
Egypt was a high culture even in European constructions.

Furthermore, Hegel is definite in his opinions about the supremacy of the Germanic people: "Only the Germanic peoples came,
through Christianity, to realize that man as man is free and that
freedom of Spirit is the very essence of man's nature." Inherent in
Hegel's view of human nature and the role of world spirit in
human matters is the belief that there is always "a dominant
people" in whose history is the unfolding of the dominant phase
of any epoch. The characteristics of Hegel's ethnocentric mind
are seen in his presentation of the four historical worlds: Oriental,
Greek, Roman, and German. He argues, in effect, that the rest of
the world serves as an audience for the central position of each

of these cultures. I am not the first to point to Hegel's arrogantly Eurocentric view of history. In fact, this aggressively European view has been reset in Samuel Huntington's *The Clash of Civilizations* and in Samuel Howe's *Empire*. To some degree, it was attempted without much success in Mary Lefkowitz's *Not Out of Africa* because of the pushback from Black and other scholars (Huntington, 2011; Lefkowitz, 1992). Their aim, it seems, is to shore up what they see as the multiplicity of challenges to a Western domination of ideas, concepts, and realities. As children of Hegel, they are attempting to strengthen walls that had already begun to decay during the renaissance of Africa and other parts of the world.

The key to an adequate analysis of Hegel's posture on history is his prosecution of an ethnocentric perspective as if it were universal. To claim, as he did, that Africa, the birthplace of human civilization was devoid of morality and therefore ahistorical demonstrated both an aggression against and an ignorance of Africa. Granted that at the time of Hegel's first lectures, Europeans did not understand the full significance of the African continent in the evolution of human society and paleontology; however, the lack of humility in the face of this ignorance is without defense.

AWARENESS OF THE RULE QUESTION

Human beings create rules. There are no rules that exist a priori: the steps to achieve this or that; the stages to reach a certain goal; or the classification of objects are all indications of human cognition. Michel Foucault and Thomas Kuhn argued that systems of thought are essentially the products of rules, but Afrocentrists are clear that rules are made by humans (Foucault, 1977; Kuhn, 1996). This fact becomes evident to those who reflect on the meaning of methodology, the philosophy of methods, and social relations, and how we relate them to other humans.

There can be no either-or positions that are taken on every issue and in science, philosophy, history, sociology or Africology. Our poverty of Afrocentric theory often leads to a pernicious scarcity in methods and rigid doctrines that endanger human freedoms. As Afrocentrists, we must retain the highest ethical standards in our methods and analysis. I once wrote that what we have seen with the end of European rationality is the Enslavement, the Holocaust, the creation of apartheid in South Africa, the dropping of murderous atomic bombs on Hiroshima and Nagasaki, the murder of Bosnian Muslims in Sbrenica, the genocide of the Tutsis in Rwanda, the ethnic cleansing of the Darfurians by the Islamic Khartoum regime, the decades old repression, suppression, and oppression of the Palestinians by the Israeli government, the Christian American building of concrete and steel walls between human beings at the Mexican border, and other rational acts! Beyond this, however, is the matter of strict systems of thought that engender either-or positions. The real poverty exists in the tradition that pits historicism against ahistoricism, structuralism against deconstruction, men against women, LGBTQ+ against heterosexuals, white against Black, etc. These are illusions built into our response patterns by the contemporary emphasis on either-or situations.

The Africological method is non-anarchic but yet stresses creativity, wishes, and intuitions rather than the strict method and authorial practice of European science. The Afrocentrist has never abandoned the position that knowledge must be sought in every human encounter with self, nature, and the cosmos. Knowledge cannot simply be counted or reduced to numbers. Everything is available to those who have the sensitivity to separate sense from nonsense.

Africology advances on all fronts simultaneously. It does not deny rationalism its historical place, but neither does it deny other forms of human inquiry about their place in the acquisition of knowledge. Human beings can reason without lessons in logic and can learn without being instructed. To advance knowledge, the fundamental ingredients must be openness to all possibilities, freedom of thought, evaluation of all data received by the human person, and the integration of all methods advanced by human beings into intellectual inquiry. Methods of history, literary criticism, history of science, botany, economics, zoology, biology, politics, physics, astronomy, medicine, and law are not necessarily contradictory and cannot be dismissed as unimportant in the search for understanding the human condition.

They must be criticized, however, for their exclusion of the "other," for their construction of an either-or paradigm, and for their anti-feminist posture. Thus, in the context of Africology most of the European-derived sciences and arts have histories of treating Africans and African contributions as irrelevant to knowledge acquisition. Such arrogance stands at the door to most fields of European studies, although the situation is slowly changing because of the impact of Afrocentric thinking on Western social sciences. Any examination of religion, for example, will show that few American or European books on religion give as much weight to African religion as to Judaism, Christianity, Islam, Hinduism, and Buddhism. This is the case although Africans were the first people recorded to have a concept of religion. No other people named the "gods" before Africans! Who called the names Ptah, Ra, Atum, and Amen, as Almighty before Africans? Furthermore, at least one African religion, Yoruba, has grown into an international religion with more than 100 million adherents.

One must often use different sensibilities to gain access to knowledge; these sensibilities give Afrocentric methods greater absorption capacities. If we examine history, we must also discard some of the traditional patterns of asking questions to obtain knowledge. Therefore, to determine how the hospitality shown to Europeans by members of King Ansah's Fante royal family in Ghana in 1482 was misunderstood, the scholar applies a multiplicity of methods while maintaining the essential core Afrocentric perspective. Cultural differences, by which I mean those values and customs that identify people in a particular manner, demonstrate how understanding and misunderstanding happen. Something as simple as buying and selling could be differently understood, especially when people have conflicting values about something like land. Europeans often thought they "bought" land from Africans or indigenous Americans for a few trinkets when in fact many of those societies did not believe that land could be bought and sold.

This means looking at the encounter between the Fante and the Portuguese from the standpoint of the Fante rather than the Portuguese—the relatively undiscussed as opposed to the more discussed—through the examination of oral traditions, linguistics, material transformation, court practices in Fante, external trade patterns as a result of the encounter, legends, myths, or any rumors found among non-Fante peoples. The Africologist advances beyond the mechanistic moment and grasps the dynamic and rhythmic process by which we live in the world. This living-in-the-world becomes the ground in which we find authentic empiricism. In this respect Afrocentric inquiry is both particular and general inquiries. It is inquiry in the sense that it engages the scholar creatively as a person who lives in the world; it is general because it operates as social inquiry encompassing psychological, cultural, and mythical dimensions of human life, thereby superseding the mechanistic model with its rather static profile.

Trained in Eurocentric perspectives, most contemporary scholars, even in Africana Studies, have only seen from a Eurocentric viewpoint and this view is decidedly different from that of the person who has been victimized by the imposition of Eurocentric expression. Afrocentricity is inevitably the philosophy of Africological scholarship in this historical moment. One cannot transcend it until it has been exhausted in its confrontation with our reality. The circumstances are uniquely social; however, it is only out of the social environment that we can derive authentic empirical experiences; otherwise, we are playing head games.

THE AFRICANIST FAILURE

The failure of the Africanists, Black or white, to make any real gains against the dominant and dominating white and Western ethos that is at the base of so many of Africa's problems is precisely due to the predicament of contradiction. These Africanists, whether Black or, as is most often the case, white, are trapped in theoretical and methodological prisons from which they can only escape with great danger to their reputations. Since they are participating in a Western enterprise and seek the accoutrements and status that come with that enterprise they must add to the store of theory or method that builds that enterprise no matter what the area of study. Therefore, an Africanist who studies the economy of Kenya, where the aim is to add to the capitalist economic theory and method, a Western enterprise, more than to the liberation of the African nation's economy from the grip of the West, is a participant in Western domination. The same can be said about the historian, anthropologist, sociologist, and linguist; only the Afrocentric scholar rises to a new level of consciousness, which claims that it is the concrete act of turning the table so that Africa assumes centrality that grants African people a new economic, historical, or linguistic vision. Indeed, we make the future by virtue of realizing in our actions the predominant objective task for restructuring the present (Keto, 1990). The authentic empirical experience is living-in-the-world with an appreciation of the individual in community as the motive force for social reconstruction. Afrocentric method approaches all African phenomena from the standpoint of

African centrality. Naturally, this centrality cannot be left to chance, but it must respond to a theoretical framework where each phenomenon is examined within the context of the authentic empiricism so fundamental to the methodology. Indeed, the quandary that Africanists, who do not read themselves as Afrocentrists, find is that they are using the same theoretical and methodological tools of Europeans who created the peripheralization of Africa. This is why the failure is devastating for those seeking to discover African agency.

The leap of imagination one finds in the best Afrocentric scholars gets its energy from the African aesthetic sensibility. What one seeks in a study is the merger of facts with beauty; this becomes the creative quest for interpretation that "looks good" while it is explaining. Any time a scholar reaches a dead end in interpretation or analysis, it is usually because he or she is utilizing the traditional methods. New discoveries will be made in authentically new ways on the edge of risk. Such studies will undoubtedly receive grudging admiration at first, but they represent the only exit from a Eurocentric, male-dominated view of the world. We are led to the Afrocentric idea of holism, everything is everything, and we are a part of the one and the other is our own measure. To begin this pilgrimage toward disentanglement will mean that we must find intellectual paths that have long been covered by the superimposition of mono-ethnic ideas as universal.

C. Tsehloane wrote in his provocative historiography, *The Africa Centered Perspective of History*, "different regions of the world that have evolved distinct cultures are entitled to develop paradigms based on the perspectives of the region's qualitatively significant human cultures, histories and experiences" (Keto, 1989, p. 15). I would say that they are not only "entitled" but that they create out of their own cultural contexts. Keto believes that a perspective called "pluriversal" can only occur by "extrapolating global rather than regional trends." Indeed, Keto believes that "the trouble at present is that studies about the rest of the world are overly influenced and often distorted by theories and conclusions drawn from studies based on a minority of the world's families, a minority of the world's women, a minority of the world's social structures and a minority of the world's cultures." (Keto, 1989, p. 15)

The insights of scholars such as Keto provide the basis for Africological theories. Here, the work of Lucius Outlaw must be considered in the philosophical context of the emergence of Africology. In fact, in his seminal 1987 paper "Africology: Normative Theory," Lucius Outlaw explains the necessity of rules governing discipline. He says, "the rules—the norms—for obtaining such agreement are not provided by melanin" (Outlaw, 1996). Outlaw underscores the position I have taken when discussing Afrocentricity because it is not simply a race-based theory of any kind; it is fundamentally about cultural agency. As a theory it is not, nor can it be based on biological determinism. Anyone willing to submit to the discipline of learning the concepts and methods may acquire the knowledge necessary for analysis.

In a sense, a revolution has already begun. Led by a host of Kemetic scholars of African origin and with the participation of several European scholars, the movement toward decolonizing information and approaches to information has touched ancient chronology, classificatory studies of civilization, African American literary studies, resistance activities of colonized and enslaved peoples, and the structure of knowledge itself. It is particularly important for us to advance a more reasonable chronology and real perspective of ancient Egypt. Lehasa Moloi's *Developing Africa?* has thrown a wrench into the normal and ordinary processes of using European methods of analysis on African phenomena. Moloi begins where all Africologists must begin, with the language itself. What is the meaning of "developing" and to what purpose is this idea of developing attached? (Moloi, 2024)

Prior to the work of Moloi, Zizwe Poe the Nkrumahist had provoked the methodological question in his provocative article, "The Construction of an Africological Method to Examine Nkrumahism's Contribution to Pan African Agency" (Poe, 2001). Poe says that his "description of Nkrumahism and Nkrumah employed a periodization that was idiosyncratic to Pan-African historiography. Descriptive theoretical tools were employed when needed from the disciplines of psychology, economics, politics, linguistics, philosophy, and international relations" (Poe, 2001). Furthermore, he claims that those tools were useful, "once calibrated, for the evaluation of broad praxis and ideology. Their use value was elevated when grounded in the life-affirming moral and ethical base of Afrocentricity" (Poe, 2001). One can see that Poe is seeking to make an advance methodologically but seems unable to completely free himself in this study from using non-Afrocentric tools. I am not saying and would never say that you should not seek compatible tools from other cultures or disciplines, that is the way of knowledge, but we must be careful that the disciplines we choose to consult are not anti-African. If we choose to use methods from other disciplines, we must truly vet the theories out of which they are derived. Thus, Poe effectively streamlines his concerns to these elements:

1. individual and organizational agency in the intellectual and social landscape;
2. psychological, political, and philosophical location;
3. historicity and hermeneutics;
4. critique and delinking;
5. denunciation of Eurocentric and Sinocentric hegemony; and
6. assertion of an African culture, personality, and genius.

Alongside the work of Zizwe Poe, we must consider the massive contribution of Victor Oguejiofor Okafor in the popular *Towards an Understanding of Africology*, the most comprehensive work carried out of the discipline itself (Okafor, 2021). Okafor suggests in chapter eight of his book that "Africological research, analysis, and synthesis are guided by three major protocols delineated in Molefi K. Asante's *Kemet, Afrocentricity, and Knowledge*" (Asante, 1990). Here, Okafor refers to the functional, categorical, and etymological paradigms. One cannot evade the use of these paradigms if one seeks to study phenomena Afrocentrically because this is how we as researchers deconstruct the racist historiography that has defined a lot of Western research. I think it is necessary to do research demonstrating the illegitimacy of traditional disciplines that support racist ideologies such as::

1. the idea that history is a totalizing discourse,
2. the idea if a universal history with Europe as the center,
3. the idea of a large chronology for locating events,
4. the idea that history is constructed around binary categories,
5. the idea that history is patriarchal, and
6. the idea that history is neutral, even innocent.

CHAPTER 2
Theoretical Grounding

To begin with, we ask the question, what are primary documents that constitute the pivot in our episteme since the creation of Black Studies in the 1960s? What was the impulse, initiated by a response to an overwhelmingly Eurocentric promotion and conceptual dominance, that started a movement? Our aim as youth who stood at the gates of universities and demanded a new curriculum was not as developed as it could have been had we been educated in the way that Carter G. Woodson had proposed in the 1930s. Yet, enough of us knew in the 1960s that we did not have to follow the path of our intellectual, spiritual, or historical death to call a halt and a make a redirection based on the principles of African knowledge and wisdom. In *The Afrocentric Manifesto*, I elaborated on the proposed five characteristics of studying Africana phenomena as a heuristic for those who would take this tradition seriously.

FIVE CHARACTERISTICS OF THE AFROCENTRIC IDEA

These were the initial five characteristics that I discovered when writing some of my earliest articles on Afrocentricity. It occurred to me afterward that the list of possible research topics is infinite; at least, to exhaust the possibilities would take considerable energy and time. Nothing prevents others from adding to this list of essential characteristics; in fact, some have attempted to do so with some success since Afrocentricity is not a received religion. I often differ with those who only assert a worldview. I do not see Afrocentricity as a worldview in the Germanic sense of the *Weltanschauung*, meaning literally world view. A researcher who approaches Africological subjects with humility, a spirit that one does not know all that one seeks to know, but is willing to listen to others, will benefit from the application of these principles.

1.   An **Interest** in psychological location: motifs, rituals, signs.
2.   A **Commitment** to Finding the subject place in any phenomenon with implications for sex, gender, class, etc.
3.   A **Defense** of African cultural element as historically valid in context of art, music, literature, based on broad responses to environment, conditions, and situations over time.
4.   A **Celebration** of centeredness, agency, and a commitment to lexical refinement, which eliminates pejorative, including sexual and gender, about Africans or other people.
5.   An **Imperative** from historical sources to revise the collective text of African people in constant search for liberation and Maat.

Furthermore, I am building upon pillars and foundations that have been laid by others. All scholarship, to establish a tradition, must indicate the grounds of its work. In my case, I accept the seven areas of Maulana Karenga's categories for the discipline: Black history, economics, communication, psychology, creative arts, social, and political issues, and would add family sciences and arts as well (Hare, 1986).

It is important to recognize the work of Serie McDougal in *Research Methods in Africana Studies* in 2014 when he wrote the first textbook devoted strictly to research in our discipline (McDougal, 2014). The philosophical work that I did in 1990 in *Kemet, Afrocentricity, and Knowledge* on the concepts of theory and method was the first book to attempt to outline how one could approach the study of data from an Afrocentric perspective. However, that book was intended to provide the first doctoral students in African American Studies with a formal presentation of the notes that I had used in the professional seminar in African American Studies after the creation of the doctoral program in 1988. It served its purpose, and the present effort is built upon many of those ideas as well as the key works by numerous other scholars such as Christian's *Philosophy and Practices for Black Studies* (2006) and Jean's book *Beyond the Eurocentric Veils* (1991). McDougal's work was a strong synthesis of the methods and approaches that were being used by the first wave of researchers in the discipline. It laid a foundation for the work that others would do in research methods (Shai, 2024).

The first aspect of theoretical grounding toward the entry into research method must be the language that is used in the project. A discipline engages data with its own peculiar language based on the established contours of the field. This is why one can discern how to approach inquiry by studying definitions. This is the first principle of study. What is it that we are trying to study, and from which angle? Afrocentricity places the African, Africa, African interests in the middle of questions of phenomena related to Africa, not on the margins, not as peripherals. Since Africology is the Afrocentric study of African phenomena transgenerationally and trans-continentally, one is ever looking to see what language confirms the centrality of African agency.

LANGUAGE OF THEORY AND METHOD

There are scores of words and terms that have emerged from more than 40 years of theorizing and research. For example, centered, centeredness, location, dislocation, phenom, markings, orientation, *djed*, relocation, frame, point, pivot, agency, agency reduction, Afronography, perspective, culture, motif, mythology, *ripoti*, margins, maaticity, periphery, African womanism, Africana womanism, indexicality, reciprocity, Eurobliviousness, plural modality, human, paradigm, myth, disorientation, subject place, *Iwa, ubuntu, maafa*, and rhythm found in the literature of the discipline. One knows from the language that is used what discipline a researcher is highlighting. The word "essentialism," for example, rarely appears in Afrocentric inquiry; it is most useful for literary critics of the Pan European Academy, often in reference to non-Europeans when, in fact, the assertive European culture has promoted the most extreme form of essentialism, white racial supremacy. Unleashing our theoretical power will have a benefit on research for beyond what we can envision, However, there are several important assumptions that the researcher must hold when starting a research project.

GENERAL AFRICOLOGICAL ASSUMPTIONS FOR RESEARCHERS

There exist elements of commonality in African Cultures

All social concepts are constructed.

Race is a constructed terminology.

Culture is a constructed terminology.

Africans are culturally similar due to geography and experiences.

Phenomena must be interpreted from an Afrocentric perspective.

Contemporary African cultures are related to ancient classical cultures.

All texts must exhibit gender sensitivity.

Afrocentric theory is not masculine-oriented or female-oriented.

Africans are subjects and agents in history.

Every phenomenon is a locus for agency.

The African origin of civilization is a scientific fact.

The monogenetic origin of the human race is unquestioned.

Research must proceed from inside of the culture.

Economic events are rooted in cultural place and position.

Afrocentricity is a critique of dominance.

The principal metaphor of analysis is location.

THREE BROAD CLASSES

Among Africologists, the study of African phenomena is primarily an examination of *cultural/aesthetic, social/behavioral*, and *policy issues*. It is generally accepted that these three knowledge areas, judiciously studied, can be used to examine all phenomena. A growing body of literature in the field suggests that serious scholarship in economics or drama, history or politics, can be classified in one of the knowledge areas. Studies are emerging around each of these cluster areas with direct interest to Africological issues. What I see is that the seven areas in Maulana Karenga's work and the research methods in Serie McDougal's work can be subsumed under one of these three classes.

A. The Cultural Aesthetic Category

By the cluster term cultural/aesthetic, one means the creative, artistic, and inventive aspect of human phenomena that demonstrates the expression of values, arts, and good. The beautiful is a subcategory of the good and is therefore not highlighted in this definition. To be good is to be beautiful according to an Afrocentric perspective. We reserve the term cultural/aesthetic for most of what is usually called in the West the arts and humanities: music, dance, literature, history, philosophy, painting, and theater. What we study in this area are the significant elements in African phenomena, whether continental or Diasporan, that give meaning to cultural character. By cultural character is meant the essence of a people's history and icons in harmonious tension. Maulana Karenga has suggested seven constituents of culture: history, religion, motif, ethos, economic, political, and social organization (Karenga, 2010). *History* is the coherent record of the achievements of a people. *Religion* or mythology is the ritualized way people present themselves to humanity. *Motif* represents the icons and symbols through which people announce themselves as human. *Ethos* is how you are projected to the world. Economic, political, and social organizations give legitimacy and power. Karenga found these concepts to be central to any discussion of culture.

A researcher might organize a study involving these key elements:

Epistemic: studying politics, ethics, psychology, *behaviors*

Scientific: studying history, linguistics, economics, *methods*

Artistic: studying symbols, icons, motifs, *types*

Despite the occasional overlapping of areas, one can find useful avenues for analytical entry into research questions. The portals are not closed; they are open, and can be expanded if necessary, utilizing the numerous nuances gathered from various other theorists and researchers, so long as one remains committed to the idea of place, location, in a cultural sense.

B. The Social Behavioral Category

On the other hand, Cheikh Anta Diop has advanced a conception of culture that includes three factors: *psychic, historic,* and *linguistic.* In his view, as seen in the *Cultural Unity of Black Africa,* the psychic factor is a mental factor; the historic deals with phenomena; and the linguistic is concerned with languages (Diop, 1989). Diop's intention is to demonstrate the unity of African culture by examining these factors. To capture Karenga's constituents while not losing sight of Diop's traditional factors, I have integrated these as including the living or dead, relationship to the cosmos, and the relationship to self. It is the area normally covered in the American system by fields such as sociology, psychology, economics, political science, urban studies, religion, and anthropology. As it is expressed in our discussion of phenomena, the social/behavioral cluster includes the critique of Eurocentric interpretations of African phenomena as well. Therefore, it is both an analysis and a criticism of the manner African social or behavioral data have been interpreted.

The criticism derives from the need to set the record straight. The idea found embedded in European thought, particularly in the 17th, 18th, 19th, and 20th centuries, that Africans were inferior socially and behaviorally has tainted most of what passes for social science in the West, definitionally and conceptually. Few have been able to escape Alexander Pope's dictum in the *Essay on Man* (1734) "some are, and must be, greater than the rest" and its implication for European contact and interpretation of that contact with the rest of the world. Stephen Jay Gould argues in *The Mismeasure of Man* that biological determinism, the idea that those perceived to be on the bottom are made of poor brains or bad genes was a shared context of European and American thinking about racial ranking (Gould, 1996). In fact, Gould contends that while racial prejudice may be as old as recorded history, "its biological justification imposed the additional burden of intrinsic inferiority upon despised groups, and precluded redemption by conversion or assimilation" (Gould, 1996). Thus, it is important that Africologists critiques all forms of discrimination based upon phenotypical, linguistic, or religious differences. Our discipline, of all disciplines, stands ready to disentangle human knowledge from all forms of mental and physical oppression. The publication of Charles Darwin's *The Origin of the Species; the Preservation of the Favorite Races,* in 1859, and his subsequent 13 years of publications devoted to expanding and applying his notion of natural selection, which can be shown persuasively to be an oxymoron, the combining of two contradictory terms without reducing the tension between them to form a new concept. Indeed, Darwin worked within the general anti-African canon while at the same time attempting to state a theory of evolution that was against the intellectual wisdom of the day (Asante & Dove, 2021).

We have to question Eurocentric empiricism's need for prediction. Most of the so-called experimental works seek to help determine human behavior and that is why predictability lies at the core of the process. What is the meaning of prediction if it is not to program one person or group to defeat another? I am not the one who would deny the right or in some cases perhaps the need for predictability, but for the Afrocentrist this should not be our approach to humanity. Greg Carr has written wisely about what Black Studies is not (Carr, 2021). There has always been something in the nuances, the serendipity, and the unexpected that moves us closer to the understanding of each other. In ethnography, that worst of all anthropological disciplines because it was meant to study the "primitive" peoples and cultures, one sees the absolute failure of ethnography to make any difference in the doctrine of white racial domination. This is why we have abandoned it for Afronography, simply the description, study, and writing about African cultures. One must also be careful that in cartography and geography we do not reuse the biases that have been taught by Europe because they are fraught with many theoretical and methodological pitfalls as well. We noticed this with the Mercator map that distorts the actual space dimensions of continents, for example, in deference to the northern hemisphere so that a country like Greenland seems larger than South America, and Russia seems larger in area than Africa.

C. The Policy Issue Category

One of the most significant categories for Afrocentric research remains policy issues because, in this area, one finds the most consequential actions for or against entire communities of people. In one of the more impressive statements about racism, the famous author Ibram X. Kendi claims that policies are critical to the life chances of African people. Personal racism is dangerous, but it becomes tragically much more catastrophic when it is embraced by a policy against entire communities. One can study political actions as tools of oppression or liberation, for example. Afrocentrists such as Carm Almonor and Valerie Harrison have studied large impacts of political decisions on educational and economic interests of African Americans (Almonor, 2023; Harrison, 2014). In one study, Latif Davis examined policies related to gun control and gun violence in a large urban community (Davis, 2024). Whenever there is a problem that needs to be resolved in the context of community, this should be seen as a policy issue that can be examined from an Afrocentric perspective using the proper tools of analysis. One expects Africologists to raise different order questions than ordinary scholars operating in the Eurocentric paradigm where the language and concepts have already been baked into the operation. We know, for example, that there are certain requirements for neoliberal or Marxist analyses because the established protocols are defined and insisted upon by the practitioners of those methods of study in our case, although we have certain language, scopes, boundaries, and concepts we are always expanding and exploring innovations in Afrocentric thought.

Ibram Kendi, of Howard University, and author of *How to be an Antiracist* understood that policies sit at the door to all intercultural and interracial issues (Kendi, 2019). Of course, he knows, and admits, that individuals bear in their own souls the burden of their cultural orientations and act on the basis of personal likes and dislikes. But as Kendi believes, this is only a small problem of our society. It is when a collective of individuals, say, of like minds, come together and create policies that discriminate against other people that we truly have the barriers to humanity. He is rightly concerned that policies have the ability to define, regulate, articulate, persecute, and isolate human beings.

Carm Almonor, the prize-winning scholar, who teaches at Princeton, believes that we have to unravel and dismantle the framework that has been constructed against African people. He sees problems around governmental regulations, educational policy, and other areas where personal prejudices have been codified into law. In fact, in 2023, he wrote "Codified Culture: An Afrocentric Diopian Public Policy Framework for Multi-Culturocracy" as a dissertation (Almonor, 2023). The aim as indicated in his subtitle was to eradicate the Patriarchal and Material Racial Ladders within K-12 Education. What Almonor argued was that employment and prison pathways were determined by policies that were set even before the children entered the educational system.

Therefore, an Afrocentrist must approach policy issues with the same clearheaded understanding of African narratives as in other areas. In fact, one must study the areas to determine what has already been done, survey the literature in our own discipline to see that others have or have not written of the issue, and then enter the topic as someone who is looking intensively for any sign of African agency. What have African people done in this situation? What elements in society encourage group solutions to this problem? How best can be save the African people and other people in our process?

Our aim must not be research for the beauty of our method, but the beauty of our methods should suggest our commitment to a protocol that would lead toward human freedom. This must be a constant part of the process for the Africologist. What is the aim of our research? And in whose interest is this research?

CHAPTER 3
Methodological Relevance

All methods of doing research have philosophical roots with specific assumptions about phenomena, human inquiry, and knowledge. The Africanist's frame of reference has too often been Eurocentric, that is, flowing from a conceptualization of African people developed to support the Western version of Africa (Cannon-Brown, 2013). The problem exists because so much of the Western tradition is firmly grounded in Hegel's conception of history. Hegel elaborated three histories or three ways of writing history: original, reflective, and philosophical. Original history, such as that of Herodotus and Thucydides, describes actions, events, and conditions that the historian saw with his own eyes or received reports of from others.

These primary historians are concerned with "what is actual and living in their environment." Such a history is a contemporary report of events and conditions. In Hegel's sense of original history, certain sociologists or anthropologists might be said to be historians. Reflective history may be universal, pragmatic, critical, or fragmentary. In its so-called universal form, it seeks to survey an entire people, country, or the world. Hegel sees problems with this method of history, chief of which is the remarkable ability of some historians to not transfer their contemporary frame of mind to the period they are writing about at the moment. Thus, he describes a Livian history that makes Roman kings and generals speak in the manner of lawyers of the Livian era and not in the traditions of Roman antiquity. The pragmatic form allows the historian to write about the past events at a present time; the confluence of events and conditions assists in nullifying the past, and therefore, all periods of history, in spite of themselves, must decide within and in accordance with its own age. Fascinated by the idea of spirit, Hegel does not count reflective history valuable unless it is history committed to exploring the deep patterns of a people. Hegel's condemnation of German-reflective histories is not that they did not follow the French example of creating a present for themselves and referring the past to the present condition.

Critical history is the evaluation of historical narratives and examples for their truth and trustworthiness. The key contribution of this method is in the ability of the author to extract results from narration rather than events. Although Hegel is content to isolate this form as a part of the reflective method of history, he is critical of it as history. Historiography, for example, could not rightly be called history, and higher criticism was itself suspect because of what Hegel sees as its "subjective fancies" replacing definite facts.

The third Hegelian method of history is philosophical. He finds the need to justify this type of historical method because unlike the cases of the original and reflective histories the concept is not self-explanatory. The Hegelian concept of philosophical history is the thoughtful contemplation of history since data of reality. This he contrasts to philosophy that allegedly produces its own ideas out of speculation, without regard to given data.

Let me be clear since I have written about Hegelian misrepresentation of Africa. He is not the only European thinker to have done so, but he is at least the writer who builds upon a certain Eurocentric idea of exclusion in a way that both attracts and repels other Europeans. They are not all the same, and no group of people are all the same. Nevertheless, the Afrocentric critique of the wall largely based on the European philosophical tradition is that Dialectic itself is problematic for the African cultural experience. So, who is willing to put up with contradictions, and for how long and to what end? I suggest that whatever we achieve as Africologists we will be more modest in trying to build entire systems based upon one particular idea. Are we truly able to consider the *unprethinkable* beingness of humanity? If so, where in African chronology is this beingness? I would hope that as we move to create a workable format for achieving our aims that we do not arrive at a predatory theory where one devours all cultures. I am buoyed by the developments in the realm of speculative arts and sciences because I am certain that our notions of Black speculative traditions and futures cannot be contained in the exclusive, arbitrary, and coercive systems sustained by fortress Europe and Arabia when you largely consider what is happening in Africa. Where is the African-speculative ambition in Sudan, Mali, Niger, Chad, for example? Who prevented its development, and why was this done? One way to achieve our aims is to use description.

Critics may assume that objectivity is compromised when the investigator uses the descriptive mode for Afrocentric research. The Afrocentrist is skeptical of the European concept of objectivity because it is invalid operationally. Marimba Ani is correct to evaluate the concept of "objectivity" negatively in her brilliant essay on European culture. I have argued that what often passes for objectivity is a sort of collective European subjectivity.[1] Therefore, it may not serve any useful purpose to speak of objectivity and subjectivity as this division is artificial in and of itself. The Afrocentricist speaks of research that is ultimately verifiable in the experiences of human beings, the final empirical authority. Of course, the methods of proof are founded upon the principles of fairness and openness. Both concepts are based on the idea of doing something that can be shown to be fair in its procedure and open in its application. What is unconscionable is the idea that when a person makes any decision that the decision is "objective", every decision, even one's choice of software for her or his word processor, is human and consequently "subjective."

One cannot conduct an authentic debate on the political philosophies of Jefferson, Hume, or Locke without a discussion of their doctrines of racial supremacy, sexism, exploitation of other nationalities, colonialism, and slavery. The genuine scholar must seek to assess the views of the political theorists considering the cultural, racial class, and gender context. The point is, no field of human knowledge can be divorced from its author's involvement as a human being in each context.

Some critics assume that the investigator may rely too much on her opinions in collecting data from a social context with which the investigator is familiar. The Afrocentric method proposes the dual-collection paradigm to deal with that problem particularly as it relates to what may be cross-cultural or cross-national research projects. This is important because in too many cases

---

[1]Marimba Ani, *Yurugu: An African Centered Critique of European Cultural Thought and Behavior* (Trenton: Africa World Press, 1994). In addition to her work objectivity, Marimba Ani created the term "Cultural Science" to replace archaeology. She proposed the term to describe a holistic method of research that applies the use of history, oral history, and various scientific methods to date and analyze cultural materials obtained while conducting research focused on human activity.

the Eurocentric method allows an individual researcher to conduct research alone. In many cases in Africa, graduate students
from American and European universities conduct research in
communities that they have little in common with and expect to
be able to make sense out of without assistance. This is probably
one of the biggest sins of the Eurocentric methods. These students assume they can ensure "objectivity" and make some sense
out of what they discover in African communities. If accurate
results are obtained it is often by default and luck not because of
some objective method.

DUAL RESEARCHERS

Two directives are invoked whenever the Africological
researcher seeks to make a cross-cultural or transracial study.
(a) The use of two researchers to collect similar data, at least one
of whom must be from the social or cultural context and (b) the
assessment of the data by two evaluators, at least one of whom
must be from the social or cultural context. In addition to the use
of the dual-collection model, researchers using the descriptive
approach will also employ triangulation of information and in-
depth interviews.

The nomothetic model of experimental laboratory research that
insists variable control and manipulation can assist in universal
laws is highly questionable. "Universal" is again one of those
Eurocentric terms that has little meaning in the real world. People
live in societies and operate within cultures. The aim of the
descriptive researcher has to be the in-depth knowledge of a
socio-human context in order to be able to make some sense out
of it, to appreciate it, and to live in peace with it. This is counter
to the experimental framework that is based on the logic of prediction, war, and the market. What is the need for the universal
idea, the control and manipulation of variables, and the predictive

ability of the researchers? Based on the war game model, the Eurocentric social scientists went to the boards and to computers to be able to predict human behavior under adverse circumstances. Particularly, advertising interests have now used this model in market research, to sell more products to African and Asian nations. The Afrocentric method must have a different goal; it must find its reason to be in the harmonizing mission. This is an interactive model rather than a distant, sterile, abstract, isolated, and noncontact model. Rather, this method finds its strength in the cooperative and integrative function of human experiences.

Edmund Husserl's *Ideas: General Introduction to Phenomenology* (1931) provoked discussion around the issue of methodology in European social sciences. Husserl's introduction of phenomenology was a major advance for Europe, but it did not settle the question of African reality. In fact, taking many of his ideas from continental African philosophy, Husserl posited a holistic view rather than a detached, isolated, disparate reality. The phenomenologist's search for essence by questioning all assumptions about reality is like the Afrocentricist's search for essence by questioning all assumptions about reality that are rooted in a particularistic view of the universe. This was pointed out to me when I argued for the doctoral program in African American Studies at Temple University. The leading phenomenologist was the first on the Graduate Committee to understand what I was describing. The distortion of social reality by traditional Eurocentric scientific methods occurs because of allegiance to a set of false assumptions. This is true whether we call the outcome of this way of viewing reality *postcolonialism, decolonial,* or *Orientalism.* Without beginning with the African origin of humanity and civilization, one cannot perform an adequate study of reality. In fact, no periodization of Africa that makes the term "colonial" central to its history is useful to the Africologist.

The Afrocentric method shares some of the perceptions of the so-called ethnomethodology but differs in both its philosophical base and its conceptualization. What it shares with ethnomethodology is the idea that reality is a process and that the discussion of normative patterns cannot be made intelligently unless the researcher understands the social context. What I have difficulty with is the Eurocentric foundation of Harold Garfinkel's view. Although Garfinkel argued correctly that researchers should not assume common meaning is shared, he incorrectly assumed that the structure that accounted for subjects' perceptions was above and beyond the contextual meaning of their culture.

But the principal problem with ethnomethodology is its Eurocentric bias. What is ethnomethodology conceptually but the white Western Eurocentric researcher saying to other white Western Eurocentric researchers "We ought to study these other people from their own contexts?" "Ethno" is derived from the medieval English "ethnic" and the Late Latin "ethica," which means "heathen." Since the Eurocentric writers did not initially include white people in their conceptualization, one can only speculate that ethnomethodology, like ethnomusicology, was meant to study those who were not Europeans.

A part of our growing consciousness is propelled by the Hegelian model for what he would call reflective history because it claims in its arrogance to be abstractive and therefore universal with the possibility of establishing a world history. Hegel's metaphysics, the principal introduction of metaphysics for the Western world, comes out in his notions of guides of the soul, the idea is in truth, the spirit, rational, and necessary will. It is impossible to understand Hegel's concept of reflective history without knowing that for him history is really spirit performing in time, as nature is idea in space. Hegel's claim was that Africa was no part of this process. As he dispensed with Africa irrationally, Africa must dispense with the Hegelian ideas of the West rationally because they are inherently anti-African and lead to various forms of theoretical and methodological distortions, often turning African scholars against their own intellectual traditions.

For the Africologist, Afrocentricity is the centerpiece of human regeneration. It challenges and takes to task the perpetuation of white racial supremacist ideas in the imagination of the African world, and by extension, the entire world. To the degree that it is incorporated into the lives of the millions of Africans on the continent and in the Diaspora, it has become revolutionary, attacking the very falsifications of truth and attitudes of self-hatred that have oppressed a great many of us.

The Africologist who wishes to research without Afrocentricity as a key underpinning is a matter of great concern for the discipline. Instead of looking out from the African's center, the non-Afrocentric person operates in a manner that is negatively predictable. The researcher's language, images, symbols, procedures, and approaches to data should advance our body of knowledge and discipline development. I propose that all researchers remember to follow these steps.

1. Looking for vital questions, formulating them clearly.
2. Gathering and assessing relevant information, using grounded metaphors to interpret effectively.
3. Completing the research with well-reasoned conclusions and solutions; testing them against historical and cultural standards.
4. Being open-minded within alternative systems of thought, recognizing and assessing assumptions implications and practical consequences of Afrocentric or non-Afrocentric actions.
5. Communicating with others, including critics, respectfully to figure out complex problems.
6. Being self-directed, self-monitored, and self-disciplined to be self-corrective as a form of authentic empiricism.

One of the early Afrocentrists, Ruth Reviere, took a scientific look at research methodology used by Europeans to study Africans. Reviere was born in St. Vincent and educated in the Caribbean, after which she left for the United Kingdom to read physics at the University of Manchester. On completion of her bachelor's degree, she returned to St. Vincent and taught there for several years, returning to the United Kingdom in 1986 to read for a Master of Science degree in physics at the University of Liverpool. Afterward, she went to Nova Scotia and completed the PhD at Dalhousie University in Halifax. As a professor at the University of the West Indies at Cave Hill, she tackled the issue of research methodology used to study the social sciences, especially those methods that were related to Africans. It is out of these experiences that she understood that by using the kiSwahili language to name her Afrocentric concepts she was exercising a measure of self-assuredness in the power of African languages to speak in ways that added to research. In this regard, she was following the proven path of the pioneer philosopher Maulana Karenga who argued in the 1960s that African people needed to master African languages and that every African language had the capacity to become a research language. Therefore, Ruth Reviere identified the fundamental concepts in her method with kiSwahili words: for example, *Ukweli,* groundedness; *Uhaki,* fairness; *Kujitoa,* structure; *Utulivu,* harmony; and *Ujamaa,* community. She had begun the process of conceptualizing her projects in terms of African languages. What Reviere revealed to other Africologists was the power of using one's own language to speak of the process of research methodology. We see this happening now among Yoruba, Igbo, Zulu, Shona, Wolof, and Xhosa philosophers. I suspect that there will be further developments in this regard leading to a common lexicon of African terms for theoretical and methodological entry.

In her article, "Toward an Afrocentric Methodology," Ruth Reviere challenged the Eurocentric fortress straightaway with "The central thesis of this article is that the traditional Eurocentric research criteria of objectivity, reliability and validity are inadequate and incorrect, especially for research involving human experiences" (Reviere, 2001, p. 709). What Reviere achieved has been followed in Africa, North America, South America, and Asia. It is of importance that the Asiascentrists have advanced the critique of the Eurocentric fortress by promoting Asian cultural forms. I see their work as collaboration against academic tyranny.

I have already seen this mechanism at work in the brilliant essays and research of Yoshitaka Miike and Jing Yin, the leaders in the movement of Asiacentric communication. One has only to read their scholarship to understand that they have mastered the model that would lead to a world community of communication scholarship loosed from the stranglehold of an unnatural Western domination. I urge Afrocentrists to read Yoshitaka Miike's "Non-Western Theory in Western Research? An Asiacentric Agenda for Asian Communication Studies" in *Review of Communication* (Volume 6, 2006, – Issue 1–2, 4–31, August 2006), as well as *Communication Theory*. New York, Routledge, 2022. Jing Yin's "Rethinking Eurocentric visions in feminist communication research: Asiacentric womanism as a theoretical framework" *in the Handbook of Global Interventions in Co*, edited by Yoshitaka Miike and Jing Yin, leaders in the movement to rethink the framework for the discipline of communication.

CHAPTER 4
Cultural Transformation

The aim of scholarship in Africology must be cultural transformation toward creating a new life for self and others. Not only must the researcher study culture, but the researcher must accept African cultural values as necessary for inquiry. This means that we must overcome the inclinations that lead to *miseducation* and *diseducation* as explained by Mwalimu Shujaa, who described miseducation as being directed toward those who are considered leaders; diseducation, Shujaa thought, had to do with an effect of distortion directed to the masses of African people (Shujaa, 1994). Both *miseducation,* as Carter G. Woodson knew (1933), and *diseducation,* as Shujaa emphasized had to be dispensed with. Our goal must be to question all assumptions about reality that are rooted in particularistic views of the universe. A cultural transformation leading to an understanding of our social and economic reality should emerge out of the collective research activities of Africologists. Every project initiated by Afrocentric scholars, those oriented to centering African reality as a principal narrative in our research, establishes the footprints for an optimistic future of discovery. Because the Africologist's goal is not prediction, but inquiry which leads to cultural transformation, it is based on three cornerstones of analysis: chronology, analogy, and demography.

Culture is the defining feature of people and nations. It is derived from years of experience, observations, ritual, science and artistic experimentation, and practices. When people have been dominated by others, it is their culture that allows them to free themselves because they are acting self-consciously in their own interests. Our research methods must allow us to battle the enemy within and the enemy without bringing about the revolution that leads to progressive cultural transformation because no culture is static. All cultures are dynamic. The enemy within is self-doubt, "dislocation, mental enslavement and anti-Africanism." The enemy without is what Michael Tillotson calls the "agency reduction formations" meant to keep us from succeeding in transformations. Our discipline stands at a crucial time in the history of knowledge because we can close the gap caused by the overwhelmingly antihuman positions of neoliberal and reactionary thinkers who have sought to deny Africans, Asians, indigenous people of the Americas and the Pacific, Mexicans, and immigrants to Western nations, the freedoms that others enjoy. All attacks on the oppressed, whether LBGTQ or straight, Jews or Muslim, Christians or Buddhists, must be challenged by Africologists who remain in the vanguard of human progress. There must be an epistemic transformation to make the cultural change that is essential to understanding our realities and introducing a new ethic. Epistemic transition is the idea that there is a time between modernity and where we need to be in the future that invites cultural transformation. What is clear is that Western modernity has exhausted its possibilities. There does not seem to be any recreative potentialities; it is like a water faucet that has run out of the ability to draw water. Modernity as an ambitious and revolutionary sociocultural paradigm based on a dynamic tension between social regulation and social emancipation advanced the West along the path of individual freedom but failed to establish the environment for collective regeneration. I think that the prevalent dynamic of the 16th century has by now tilted toward regulation and away from emancipation. The Trumpian Moment, for example, in American history has meant the strangulation of social and cultural freedom, and the advancement of the restrictive power of the state to control people. The collapse of emancipation rhetoric and practice symbolizes the exhaustion of Western modernity. I see then the emergence of a new approach to cultural transformation. One must also be aware of the growing importance of artificial intelligence advancements such as Latimer, a whole language model, based on Afrocentric ideas. John Pasmore, the creator of Latimer, named for the African American scientist-engineer, has pioneered Latimer to enter the market for an Afrocentric engine that would respond to all research inquiries. This is an infinite quest for data and analysis that will underwrite the future research of the most committed Afrocentrists.

EXAMPLES FOR ACTUAL RESEARCH

I will look at several recent in the field to demonstrate methodology. The first is Olumayowa Ogedengbe's "Africological Study of Western Christianity and Yoruba Society." This was the first time that an Afrocentrist Africologist examined the relationship between Yoruba and Christianity. Of course, because of European and American influences the Yoruba had been studied through Western lens. In this work, in 1995, Ogedengbe made it clear that he saw how Christianity affected Yoruba in six ways: (a) enhancing the individualistic ethos, (b) destroying family and communal bonds, (c) promotion of Yoruba cultural illiteracy, (d) mystification of Yoruba values, (e) metropolitization of Yoruba in a supra-Christian culture, and (f) shifting Yoruba to the fringes of the Christian culture. So, Ogedengbe wrote that he would use an "Africological method of inquiry," which would employ an amalgam of functional, categorical, and etymological paradigms (Ogedengbe, 1995). Quoting Asante, he writes "the *functional* paradigm represents needs, policy, and action ... the *categoral* paradigm refers to issues of schemes, gender, class, themes, and files. The *etymological* paradigm deals with language, particularly in terms of word and concept origin" (Asante, 1990, p. 12).

Carm Almonor's "A Cultural and Historical Public Policy Framework for Multi-Peopled Democracy" sought to establish an Afrocentric critique and assertion in the arena of public policy. Almonor wrote in this fashion: "I first witnessed signs of what I have come to view as *compulsory institutional dislocation* as the volunteer curriculum director of a boys after school program in Central New Jersey. My students arrived from vastly different school settings and grade levels ranging from K-12, yet almost universally shared similar reflections about their classrooms. Most had found little schoolbook inspiration for employment goals beyond football, basketball and rapping. Few had ever had a Black male teacher to model their role in education or in socially ordered behavior, a trend exacerbated by their mostly fatherless homes." Here Almonor saw the nature of the school and classroom based upon his in-depth Afrocentric study of institutions.

In another instance, one can also gather an Africological approach from Carmella Harris's emphasis on memory in the study of Harriet Tubman. Harris states that the methodology used in her dissertation "is Afrocentric in the sense that I am seeking to discover how African American people have viewed the role of Harriet Tubman in history. This is not merely a study of Harriet Tubman's life, but rather an examination of her public memory in the lives, experiences, and ordinary pursuits of

African Americans. Consequently, although I will, of necessity, use materials that were created by some writers and memorialists who were European, I shall examine the production of their work through the eyes of African people. For example, if a statue of Harriet Tubman exists, I would like to discover not only the creator of the statue but the public record of responses to the statue. As an Africologist, I seek to make an Afrocentric inquiry into the historical phenomenon of Harriet Tubman from the standpoint of African people's agency. What, for example, is the purpose of Tubman's representation in poetry, narratives, oratory, paintings and sculptures?" While I see these as important questions to probe for Afrocentric clarity, the researcher must also submit procedures that will support the overall objective.

Harris understands, following Asante's work, "that location is a principal arena for Afrocentric discovery. Where is the creator of an object located, or where is the viewer, or user of an object located culturally or psychologically?" (Harris, 2024). Procedurally, the researcher must amass data, collect texts, memorials, letters, and any physical evidence required to begin the inquiry. Of course, as Harris states the researcher must know where she is located psychologically, culturally, or historically. To be an Afrocentric researcher one must not examine data from the standpoint of only European eyes; one must fight against the laziness that allows us to fall back on what we have been taught. Our aim, as rebel intellectuals, is to break the chains that hold our thoughts, interpretations, and analyses in perpetual check. Until the hunted learns to hunt, they will always be victims.

Emmanuel Cudjoe did a study of the Kete dance of the royal court of the Asante in Ghana (Cudjoe, 2023). He was discouraged from writing his doctoral work on Ghanaian Royal Dance by professors who thought that he should concentrate on European theory and practice. Convinced that he could study performative arts such as dance, singing, and theater, especially if it were based on field work, that is, where one goes to the site of activities and then reports them, Cudjoe suggested that he might use the Afronographic method. His method would recognize the negative effects of colonization on African people's perceptions of self-worth and freedom. Cudjoe was adamant that "the study of knowledge systems of Africa by its own people, especially performing arts forms such as dance and music, provides multiple possibilities, including: (a) examination of non-African epistemologies and their application to African dance history and culture, (b) historical inquiry on African epistemology in the African context, (c) gradual inclusion of Afrocentric educational curriculum that places African knowledge at the center of African knowledge construction, both personal and collective, and (d) redefinition of the parameters and constituents of African knowledge to include phenomenology of African agency, in other words, first person perspectives" (Cudjo, 2023). Cudjoe presented to his doctoral committee a blended Afronography with phenomenological and hermeneutic interviewing of autoethnographic researchers informing the study design.

Michelle B. Taylor established a methodological rubric in her dissertation "*Black Mamas on the Screen: African Matriarchy and African American Motherhood in Spike Lee Joints.*" She has contributed to the development of a unique framework for analyzing films using an Afrocentric methodology and lens, specifically one that considers African matriarchy and African motherhood as focal points for analysis. Taylor created a rubric that drew on communication, history, and culture related to the lived experiences of African American mothers adding to the methodological uniqueness of her project (Taylor, 2024). She has already mastered the technique of content analysis and introduced her own innovative and original interpretative rubric for film analysis for scholarly research.

APPROACHES TO METHODS

Using Eurocentric theories and methods to explain the behavior and ethos of African Americans can be disconcerting and mis-leading. Our thinkers such as Maulana Karenga, Daryl Harris, Christel Temple, Jerome Schiele, Nah Dove, Asa Hilliard, Joyce King, and Wade Nobles have assumed the inappropriateness of Eurocentric assumptions in the study of African phenomena not because the researchers are white or Arabs, but because they seldom dare see phenomena from the perspective of African agency. Of course, there are exceptions and those have been noted in various historical, philosophical, and literary works. People like Ana Monteiro Ferreira, Elisa Nascimento, Basil Davidson, and Michael Bradley have challenged the standard fare of Eurocentric writings (Bradley, 1991; Davidson, 1984; Ferreira, 2013; Nascimento, 2008).

As I have intimated before, Africology establishes its disciplinary scope and chronological sequences based on the study of events, ideas, and personalities related to Africa, on the continent or in the diaspora. The mere study of phenomena of Africa is not Africology but some other intellectual enterprise. By now, you know that the scholar who generates research questions based on the centrality of Africa is engaged in a very different research inquiry than the one who imposes Western criteria on African phenomena.

African experiential culture and history determine all inquiry: the right questions to ask, and the right way to answer them. Moreover, emotion and reason are complements to physical data; holistic subject immersion is necessary and might even engage extrasensory, intuitive measures to constitute valid infor-mation sources. We know enough to understand that all interpretation is not contained in the canons of European thought. This is why, alongside Nah Dove, we have proposed a *prohuman* methodology in our book, *Being Human Being:*

Transforming the Race Discourse (Asante & Dove, 2021). This is not a prehuman method nor a de-human idea, but rather the idea that our methodology must engage as much of humanity's possibilities as we can to understand our universe. Afrocentric theory demands a discourse that privileges African reality, but it also needs methods and procedures that are grounded in the human being (McDougal, 2017). McDougal's work introduced us to the possibilities within our discipline and laid a foundation for further advances.

Michael Tillotson created a methical utility that he defined as Agency Reduction Formation. According to Tillotson (2011), "(ARF) is any ideological tool that distracts, neutralizes or reduces the need and desire for assertive collective agency by people of African descent." As forms of ideological domination, Tillotson argues iterations of ARF distort reality to reinforce oppressive systems while influencing less anti-egalitarian political practices. ARF, according to Tillotson, stems from six unresolved epochs of oppression that continuously contribute to compromising agency: *colonialism, enslavement, Jim Crow, Apartheid, de facto*, and *de jure* segregation (Tillotson, 2011, p. 60). These epochs manifest themselves differently throughout the world; however, they are collaboratively connected to enduring problems associated with the reduction in human agency.

AFRONOGRAPHY

Afronography is the writing of African qualitative research. It centers the African experience and bends toward human ends and values, utilizing qualitative investigations. It is like ethnography in its procedures, but it does not start from the same source. Ethnography assumed a Eurocentric worldview and created a discipline to study everyone except Europeans. It became, in its practice, perhaps one of the most racist of research pursuits because it constantly constructed the world of the "other" as opposed to the common humanity one sees in Afrocentricity.

The best way to think of Afronography is that it is an Afrocentric description that systematically records and reports phenomena of a personal and collective nature to gain a cultural understanding of society. Afronography is not the same as ethnography, which emphasizes an analysis that looks at ethnicity and the illusory category of race; rather, it is a culturally conscious way of doing research. A researcher can use elements of memoir, autobiography, social contexts reports, and interviews. Dove's book, *Afrikan Mothers: Bearers of Culture, Makers of Change*, represents one of the first examinations in the discipline of Africology to challenge the canonical methods of approaching African women (Dove, 1998). In fact, the scholar Kariamu Welsh Asante wrote the blurb on the cover of the book, "Nah Dove's text is tender, full of grace, and gentle even as she weaves a powerful and mighty pen in a solid cultural analysis, Afrikan Centered perspective, and in-depth research. Dr. Dove's commitment to the struggle is evident in her loving description of the women that she profiles and her respectful discussion of their lives and choices for their children. Dr. Dove speaks as an Afrikan mother, activist, and scholar and this combination infuses her work with humility and conviction. Nah Dove is to be commended for this gift to all bearers of cultures. Her wisdom makes her one of 'the women who gather at the grindstones'" (Welsh quoted on back of Dove, 1998). Cudjoe discovered what Dove understood by her own research mainly in Ghana, and that was that data discovery could arise at any time during a visit to villages, the royal courts, or in homes. A moment of observation of an incident, a movement, an occupation, or the presence of a particular personality can call for Afrocentric reflections.

Using Dove's construction of *Maaticity* as the ultimate objective of good research, the researcher who sees to transform society looks for order, balance, harmony, justice, righteousness, truth, and reciprocity, constituted as the search for *Maaticity*. A keen observer is looking for all effects, reflections, and transcendence to combine ancestral, historical, and artistic wisdom to bear on any research situation.

These elements of inquiry operate inextricably as one, as a documentary narrative, with its statistical data context, and its ethical use for social change mutually informing one another. In fact, our axiological compass must properly guide our epistemological pursuits, or our greatest human discoveries can become the most destructive tools of hierarchical inhumanity.

This is precisely the reason I always start with classical Kemetic knowledge; this is a serious orientation to African origin (Bernal, 1987; Obenga, 1996). It allows the researcher to make clear the philosophical, reflective, and moral basis of all epistemologies: It clarifies life purpose and thereby meaning and remains moored in Maaticity. When one becomes a sage researcher, which is the top category of Afrocentric scholars, they will have mastered the fundamental elements of classical Nile civilizations and will have learned how they all flow from the same source (Diop, 1974; Hilliard, 1995). Our aim is also one, the achievement of Maaticity in our work, lives, and legacies, all borne on the backs of good Afrocentric research methodology.

CHAPTER 5
Literary Analysis

Although I developed the theory of Afrocentricity in the late 1970s and early 1980s, it was not until Katherine Bankole, one of my graduate students, explored the idea of establishing a comprehensive glossary of Afrocentric terms in the 1990s. One can imagine that it was limited at the time but it was the right effort to draw lines in the sand around the idea of Africology. Bankole-Medina has gone on to create many contributions to the discipline by advancing her own research using the techniques found in our corpus.

Bankole-Medina is the author of many scholarly publications including the groundbreaking text (Bankole, 2017). Her paper, "In the Age of Malcolm X: Social Conflict and the Critique of African American Identity Construction" appears in James L. Conyers, Jr. and James Smallwood's, *Malcolm X: A Historical Reader* (Baltimore, MD: Carolina Academic Press, 2008). She published several entries in the *Encyclopedia of African Religion* (edited by Molefi Kete Asante and Ama Mazama), and book reviews including a review of slavery and botanical medicine for the *Journal of Southern History*. Building on her previous work as the Historical Consultant for *Caminho De Sao Tome: A Documentary on Cape Verde*, she published the chapter "Mulheres Africanas Nos Estados Unidos," in *Afrocentricidade: Uma Abordagem Epistemologica Inovadora* (Sankofa: Matrizes Africanas Da Cultura Brasileira 4 by Elisa Larkin Nascimento, Sao Paulo, Brasil: Selo Negro Edicoes, 2008). In 20th century African American history, her articulation of the life and legacy of Charles Hamilton Houston appears as chapters and articles. Dr. Bankole-Medina is the founding editor of *Africalogical Perspectives*, a scholarly journal, and the senior editor of *Women of African Descent and Justice in World Societies* (with Dr. Abena Lewis-Mhoon and Prof. Stephanie Yarbough).

A scholar who followed Bankole-Medina in Afrocentric research was Christel Temple, the editor of the prestigious *Journal of Black Studies* since 2021. She introduced important research tools and ideas for the study of African and African America literature. Anyone who seeks to apply Afrocentric ideas to the analysis of literature is lost without Christel Temple's intellectual guidance. She remains the leading Afrocentric literary scholar by virtue of boldly applying the core principles of our discipline orientation to texts. I remember wondering several years ago when a literary-oriented scholar would be brave enough to abandon the endless Eurocentric debates about deconstruction, structuralism, and reception theory and create out of our own understanding of literature. This is where both Bankole-Medina and Temple have led us.

There are three important theoretical tools that are essential for the person doing literary or artistic analysis.

BLACK CULTURAL MYTHOLOGY

Black Cultural Mythology, according to Christel Temple, is a framework of analysis that infuses hero dynamics, legacy tools, heritage practices, and ancestor acknowledgment in Black literature and cultural behaviors. These practices include holidays, folk tales, monuments, and commemorations. Temple argues these practices are especially important in regions where Black people are fewer in population, and in regions where the national histories of enslavement lean on the institutionalized patterns of selective memory. These stories of hyper-heroic survivalist behaviors become philosophies on survival, resilience, and commemoration; and as a form of cultural memory, they become a shared transatlantic feature of diasporic African remembrance.

Christel Temple speaks of Black Cultural Mythology as an analytical instrument that can be used in defining the relationship between public sculpture, storytelling, and cultural memory (Temple, 2020). The scholar must know that monuments and buildings reaffirm multiple aspects of mythology. Temple affirms that monuments and public sculptures reflect one of the highest forms of historical writing because with one's own sense of art and aesthetics, one can reinforce the values and views of generations of ancestors (Temple, 2020). From a theoretical perspective, Temple's discussion of Black Cultural Mythology acknowledges how events such as the Haitian Revolution reflect epic heroics, contributing to the wide mythological structure of diaspora. The richness of Black Cultural Mythology can be a challenge to most researchers. Therefore, I would suggest that the serious scholar should first undertake a comprehensive study of African and African American cultural artifacts to become acquainted with the various ways Africans have produced literature, art, and culture. Such an immersive act will allow the researcher to have a better handle on the analysis that will be made. It is sad when you see researchers who could have pulled off top notch works fail because they do not know the allusions to cultural artifacts or individuals that would make their work more robust.

There are two entries into the methodological field that support the direction of Christel Temple's work. Both are maatic in the sense that they are derivative from the overarching concepts found in Maat. The two fields are *nzuri* and *nefer*. Nzuri is a kiSwahili term that is usually translated in English as "good," or "beauty." Nefer is a Kemetic work that is usually translated in English as "good," and "beautiful" (Cannon-Brown, 2013). What these words reflect is the commonality over generations of the same African concept in different parts of the continent. Whether in ancient Egypt along the Nile or in Tanzania near Kilimanjaro the idea of beauty and good being connected remains the same. One finds the same connection throughout the African continent.

THE NZURI MODEL

The Nzuri model was promoted by Kariamu Welsh Asante as early as the 1980s, culminating in her work with the Zimbabwe National Dance Company. The Nzuri model appears in her books and articles as an approach to the study of literature, art, and culture. Among her books are *Zimbabwe Dance: Rhythmic Forces, Ancestral Voices—An Aesthetic Analysis*, and *Umfundalai: An African Dance Technique*. She was the editor of *The African Aesthetic: Keeper of Traditions* and *African Dance: An Artistic, Historical and Philosophical Inquiry*. She coedited *African Culture: Rhythms of Unity* with Molefi Kete Asante (Asante & Welsh Asante, 1990).

THE NEFER PARADIGM

The Nefer Paradigm was first suggested by Willie Cannon-Brown who articulated a powerful ethic of beauty based on an understanding of the ciKam word for beauty and good. Her book *Nefer: The Aesthetic Ideal in Egypt* was one of the first to give a direction to scholars seeking to capture the essence of African life. Cannon-Brown captures the spirit of the Afrocentric method when she writes: "Afrocentric methodology is rooted in the idea that all discussions of African history, art, culture, and motif must be centered in the context of African people." Consequently, the centrality of the African context has been established to yield an understanding of the relationship between Maat and nefer as the aesthetic ideal. After reviewing the options for gaining access to information regarding the question of beauty, the method first articulated in Asante's (1990) work, *Kemet, Afrocentricity, and Knowledge*, is necessary to provide meaning in this African project. In *Kemet, Afrocentricity, and Knowledge*, Asante suggests three key elements that make up a cultural framework which will allow a reader to discover specific aspects of African Culture; therefore, aspects of the epistemic, the scientific, and the artistic elements will be applicable in this study. According to Asante, the epistemic element includes ethics, politics, and psychology; hence, modes of behavior. The scientific element includes history, linguistics, and economics; hence, methods of investigation.

The artistic element includes icons, art, motifs, and symbols; hence, types of presentation. These three elements represent the framework for my critical analysis of the relationship between *maat* and *nefer* as the aesthetic ideal." Willie Cannon-Brown further argues that the researcher must be keen to understand the nature of the data and information. She posits that "To determine what information is conveyed by a historical text or an artistic object, the researcher must have a methodology. Moreover, to determine relations between a major concept like *maat* and *nefer* and the aesthetic ideal, it is necessary for the researcher to use methods appropriate to this discourse. Afrocentric methods permit the researcher to define the boundaries and context of the text, object, or relationship within the framework of African centrality. It also allows the researcher to find the proper tools for analysis based upon what is fundamental to African realities, thus, bringing about a richer understanding of the meaning of the object, text, relationship, or subject" (Cannon-Brown, 2013). What is required, she claims, are two assumptions:

1. The meaning of a concept is fully the product of its own historical milieu, and the contemporary researcher can only incompletely understand it.
2. Afrocentric methods deny the imposition of Eurocentric claims on African concepts by positing African ideals at the center of the investigation.

Even with these assumptions, the advocate of Afrocentric methodology would not assume that all conventional ideas could be or need to be reinterpreted with Afrocentric methodology. However, it is a fact that any information related to African people that has not been interpreted from the standpoint of Afrocentricity might contain seeds of misorientation and misinterpretation.

ANALYZING ORATORY AND RHETORIC

One of the earlier areas studied by Afrocentrists was African American oratory and rhetorical traditions. Part of the reason why discourse analyses were important had to do with the insistent demand for human rights in the United States. Although the category was called Civil Rights by the American government, the world understood African Americans to be fighting for human rights. Within the context of the American political order, it was called Civil Rights.

Nevertheless, the tradition of oratory was long and elegant in African American history and some scholars studied Sojourner Truth, Marcus Garvey, Frederick Douglass, Anna Julia Cooper, Booker T. Washington, John Pennington, Martin Luther King, Jr. Franklin Florence, Malcolm X, and numerous contemporaries. Using Afrocentric principles, what is the procedure for analyzing

African Discourse? Here are the steps that I believe the researcher must take after collecting texts, speeches, historical vignettes, social media posts, recordings, and so forth. You must then follow these procedures.

Center the orator in the middle of historical literatures and oratures of African people. This means that you will have a context, an abundance of cultural materials;

Transcend all Eurocentric negations about the particular orator or writer;

Abandon any stereotypical preoccupation;

Embrace a large structure vision of reality that allows for comparative references;

Use the three fundamental themes of transcendent discourse:

- human to the supernatural,
- human relationship to self, and
- human in relationship to community.

Address the analysis to a particular audience who might be of any age, gender, class or culture.

Employ the African cultural mythoforms, like *Shine, Stagolee, John Henry, Malindy, Nyanga, and High John De Conqueror* that inform the creative expression in oratory; and

Discuss the author/orator, and texts in relationship to liberation rhetoric and practice.

A good researcher will examine texts and other communication forms with an eye toward understanding and effectiveness. This means that the more one knows about a given African society or community, the more effective will be the analysis. Always be on the lookout for new ways, based on culture, to make analysis, tropes, and metaphors for clarity.

CHAPTER 6
Applications and Procedures

One of the immediate differences between what we do as Africologists and what is practiced in other disciplines is our insistence on discovering in the classical foundations of African culture the resources for our applications and procedures. This is the essential work of doing the fundamentals of Kemetic science and culture. Without this orientation, it will be more difficult to understand what is necessary to proceed to procedures. Let us begin by raising the highest order questions that the African mind considered at the dawn of writing. The sages, men and women, who observed the material universe and probed the depths of human thoughts and ideas, wanted to find out how we could proceed with discovery. Consequently, they asked the following:

How to show the unshowable?

How to express the inexpressible?

How to hear the inaudible?

How to measure the immeasurable?

How to describe the indescribable?

The purpose of these questions was to train the mind to ask the questions beyond the obvious question, that is, to probe the possibility that something other than what we see, feel, hear, measure, and describe exists. If it exists, then how best can we approach it? Of course, one of the ways that we have tried to close the gap between what we know and what we do not know is to develop research questions. In fact, I have chosen to call them Guiding Questions because they should lead to other questions which will give us a more robust answer to our concerns.

GUIDING QUESTIONS

Guiding questions are not mere questions for immediate data, like "Who are Shango, Oshun, and Ogun?" One could easily find the answer to this question and provide the answer from Yoruba culture that they represent orishas. But a true Guiding Question is not the one that seeks mere facts but that probes for depth. For example, one might want to ask, "Are Africans in the Americas, the Caribbean, and Europe related to the Africans on the continent?" This is a guiding question with the possibilities of leading us into the complexities of diasporas, migrations, integration, and national identities. The order of this question is different from "Who is C. Tsehloane Keto or Ruth Reviere?" Afrocentric ancestor thinkers like Keto and Reviere should be studied for their intellectual contributions because without them we would not have the plinth we are standing on. Nevertheless, a question about them biographically is really an informational question, not a guiding one for complex discussion and debate.

EXPLORATORY TOPICS FOR RESEARCH STUDY

I suggest that students in Africology might want to consider some of these topics for discussion, research, and dissertation analyses:

1. An Investigation of the Ethical Content in the works of Maulana Karenga and Lewis Gordon
2. An Examination and Comparison of the Race Pride Idea in William E. B. Du Bois and Mary McLeod Bethune
3. An Analysis of the effect of self-conscious cultural training on African American High School Students
4. An Exploration of Asa Hilliard's Ideas on Education as Significant Pointers to Transformation
5. One could analyze the origin of Joyce E. King's Cultural Constructs
6. A Study of the Revolutionary Methods of Marimba Ani and Frances Cress Welsing
7. Make a Content Analysis of Herbert Ekwe Ekwe's Afrocentricity
8. Recreate Wade Nobles' Paradigm for the Education of Young Boys
9. Place Jawanza Kunjufu and the Education of Black Boys in Historical Context
10. Reconstruct Carter G. Woodson's Plinth of African American History
11. Resolve the Tension in Toni Morrison's Novel and Afrofuturism
12. Examine Katherine Bankole-Medina's Afrocentric Conceptualization of Medicine
13. Historize and Afrocentricize George Padmore's Influence on Pan Africanism
14. Differentiate Between Biko's Assertive Blackness, Asante's Afrocentricity, Senghor's Negritude, and Karenga's Kawaida
15. Liberation Utility of Nah Dove's African Womanism and Clenora Hudson-Weems' Africana Womanism
16. Various Histories of the Disciplines, Especially Departments and Their Struggles
17. Afrocentricity and Speculative Realities in the Field of Africology

18. The Role of Intellectual Warriors: Jacob Carruthers, Asa Hilliard, Yosef Ben Johanson, Leonard Jeffries, Charshee McIntyre, and Vivian Gordon

A CRITICAL INTERROGATION OF THE AFRICAN DIASPORA

Finally, I want to provide you with a heuristic for the study of the African diaspora. I have read many books and articles about the African diaspora, but I have rarely seen an Afrocentric examination of the phenomenon. This is where critical Afrocentricity must take its place because it is the art of evaluating thinking, speaking, and writing about African phenomena with a view toward improvement in society and oneself. It is based on the Afrocentric logic with the following questions.

What is the cultural referent being used?

What constitutes the boundaries of the diaspora?

What is the main purpose of our interrogation?

What are the guiding questions?

What is the main inference/conclusion to be drawn by our research?

What are the key concepts and how will they advance our discipline?

What are the assumptions about the diaspora we are studying? Are they Afrocentric, that is, are they centered around African agency?

Following the reason and analysis, what are the implications for bringing about a more Maatic world?

AN ALTERNATIVE TEMPLATE FOR APPROACHING AN INQUIRY INTO DIASPORA

What is the fundamental purpose?

What is the fundamental problem with the diaspora?

What are the data or information that we have?

What are the inferences that can be drawn from this information?

What is the point of view? Are there different points of view?

What are the principal concepts?

What are the implications of this approach to diaspora?

STRONG AFROCENTRIC TRAITS

Ultimately, the critical interrogator will demonstrate courage, empathy, perseverance, dignity, reason, autonomy, humility, respect, and good character. As an Africological scholar, you are at best a good honest person thinking clearly beyond your own personal goals.

References

Akua, C. (2012). *Education for transformation: The keys to releasing the genius of African American students*. Teacher transformation Institute.

Almonor, C. (2023). *An Afrocentric public policy inquiry: Reducing patriarchy and hierarchy in K-12 education* [Dissertation] Temple University.

Anderson, R. (2016). *Afrofuturism 2.0: The rise of Astro-Blackness and the Black speculative arts movement*. Lexington Books.

Anderson, R. (2025). *Afrofuturism in the world order*. Ohio State University Press.

Ani, M. (1994). *Yurugu: An African-centered critique of European cultural thought and behavior*. Africa World Press.

Asante, M. K. (1987). *The Afrocentric idea*. Temple University Press.

Asante, M., & Welsh Asante, K. (Eds.). (1990). *African culture: Rhythms of unity*. Africa World Press.

Asante, M. K. (1990). *Kemet, Afrocentricity and knowledge*. Africa World Press.

Asante, M. K. (2007). *Afrocentric manifesto*. Polity.

Asante, M. K. (2020, April). Toward a transformative curriculum for higher education. *International Journal of African Renaissance Studies, 15*(1), 1–16.

Asante, M. K., & Dove, N. (2021). *Being human being: Transforming the race discourse*. Universal Write Publication LLC.

Bankole, K. (2017). *Slavery and medicine: Enslavement and medical practices in antebellum Louisiana*. Liberated Scholars Publishers.

Banks, W. C. (1992). The theoretical and methodological crisis of the Afrocentric conception. *Journal of Negro Education, 61*(3), 262–272.

Bernal, M. (1987). *Black Athena: The Afroasiatic roots of classical civilization.* Free Association Books.

Bradley, M. (1991). *The iceman inheritance.* Kayode.

Cannon-Brown, W. (2013). *Nefer: The aesthetic ideal in classical Egypt.* Routledge.

Carr, G. (2021). What Black Studies is not: Moving from crisis to liberation in Africana intellectual work. *Socialism and Democracy, 25,* 178–191.

Christian, M. (2006). Philosophy and practice for Black Studies: The case for studying White supremacy In M. K. Asante & M. Karenga (Eds.), *Handbook of Black studies* (pp. 76–88). Sage.

Clark, K. (1969). *Civilisation: The Skin of our Teeth.* British Broadcasting Corporation (BBC).

Clarke, J. (1991). *Africans at crossroads.* Africa World Press.

Cudjo, E. (2023). *From the palace to the academy: Kete Dance.* Temple Dissertation.

Davidson, B. (1984). *The Story of Africa.* Littlehampton Book Services Ltd.

Davis, L. (2024). *Gun points: The role of culture in violence.* Independently Published.

Diop, C. A. (1974). *African origin of civilization: Myth or reality.* Lawrence & Hills.

Diop, C. A. (1989). *The cultural unity of Black Africa.* Karnak House.

Dove, N. (1998). *Afrikan Mothers: Bearers of culture makers of change.* SUNY Press.

Ferreira, A. (2013). *The demise of the inhuman.* SUNY Press.

Foucault, M. (1977). *Discipline and punish: The Birth of the prison.* Vintage Books.

Gould, S. (1996). *The mismeasure of man.* Norton.

Hare, N. (1986). *The endangered black family: Coping with unisexualization and the coming extinction of the Black race.* Black Think Tank.

Harris, C. (2024). *Harriet Tubman: A narrative of agency* [Dissertation]. Temple University.

Harrison, V. (2014). *The racial significance of Pennsylvania's K-12 public funding scheme* [Dissertation]. Temple University.

Hegel, G. W. F. (1956). *The philosophy of history*. Dover.

Hilliard, A. (1995). *The maroon within us: Selected essays on African American community socialization*. Black Classic Press.

Huntington, S. (2011). *The clash of civilizations and the remaking of world order*. Simon and Schuster.

Husserl, E. (1931). *General introduction to pure phenomenology*. Routledge.

Jean, C. (1991). *Beyond the Eurocentric veils*. University of Massachusetts Press.

Jochannan, Y. B. (1972). *Black man of the Nile: And his family*. Black Classic Press.

Karenga, M. R. (2010). *Introduction to Black studies*. University of Sankore Press.

Karenga, M. (2003, Winter–Spring). DuBois and the question of the color line: Race and class in the age of globalization. *Socialism and Democracy*, *17*(1), pp. 141–160; see also Karenga, "Mission, Meaning and Methodology in Africana Studies: Critical Reflections from a Kawaida Framework," *The Black Studies Journal* (Fall/Spring) 2000–2001, 3, 54–74.

Keto, C. T. (1989). *The Africa centered perspective of history*. KA Publications.

James, G. (2017). *Stolen legacy: Greek philosophy is stolen Egyptian philosophy*. Allegro.

Kendi, I. (2019). *How to be an antiracist*. One World.

Keto, C. T. (1990). *Africa-centered perspective of history*. C. A. Associates.

Kuhn, T. (1996). *The structure of scientific revolutions*. University of Chicago Press.

Lefkowitz, M. (1992). *Not out of Africa: The origins of Greece and the illusions of Afrocentrists*. The New Republic.

Monges, M. (1995). *Kush: The Jewel of Nubia*. Africa World Press.

McDougal, S. (2014). *Research methods in Africana studies (Black Studies and Critical Thinking)*. Peter Lang Inc.

Miike, Y. (2019). Intercultural communication ethics: An Asiacentric perspective. *The Journal of International Communication, 25*(2), 159–192.

Moloi, L. (2024). *Developing Africa?: New Horizons with Afrocentricity*. Anthem.

Ndlovu-Gatsheni, S. J. (2015). Decoloniality as the future of Africa. *History Compass, 13*(10), 485–496. https://doi.org/10.111/hic3.12264

Nascimento, E. (2008). *The sorcery of color.* Temple University Press.

Obenga, T. (1996). *Ancient Egypt and Black Africa.* Lushena Books.

Ogedengbe, M. O. (1995). *An Africological Study of Western Christianity ad a Yoruba Society of Western Nigeria* [Dissertation]. Temple University.

Okafor, V. O. (2021). *Toward an understanding of Africology.* Kendall Hunt Publishing Company.

Outlaw, L. (1996). *On race and philosophy.* Routledge.

Poe, D. (2001). The construction of an Africological method to examine Nkrumahism's contribution to Pan African agency. *Journal of Black Studies, 31*(6): 729–745.

Pope, A. (1734). *An essay on man* (pp 74–78). John Wright, for Lawton Gilliver.

Reviere, R. (2001). Toward Afrocentric research methodology. *Journal of Black Studies, 31,* 709–728.

Rogers, J. A. (1972). *World's great men of color* (Vols. 1 & 2). Coller Books, Simon & Schuster.

Sesanti, S. (2019). Decolonized and Afrocentric education: For centering African women in remembering, re-membering, and the African renaissance. *Journal of Black Studies, 50*(5), 431–449.

Shai, K. B. (2024). Afrocentric epistemology for social sciences (interview). *Journal of the Institute for African Studies, 3,* 107–113.

Shujaa, M. J. (1994). *Too much shooting, Too little education: A paradox of black life in White societies.* African World Press.

Smith, A. (2023). *Afrocentricity in Afrofuturism.* University of Mississippi Press.

Taylor, M. B. (2024). *Black Mamas on the Screen: African Matriarchy and African American Motherhood in Spike Lee Joints.* Temple Dissertation.

Temple, C. (2020). *Black cultural mythology.* State University of New York Press.

Tillotson, M. J. (2011). *Invisible Jim Crow: Contemporary ideological threats to the internal security of African American.* African World Press.

Walters, R. W. (1990). *The Afrocentricity concept at Howard University: A viewpoint.* New Directions, 17, 6–9.

Williams, C. (1993). *The rebirth of African civilization.* Third World Press.

Woodson, C. G. (1933). *The miseducation of the negro.* Associated Publishers.

Index

www.ingramcontent.com/pod-product-compliance
Lightning Source LLC
Chambersburg PA
CBHW052025030426

42335CB00026B/3285